WE THE PEOPLE

A SIGNER FOR INDEPENDENCE
JOHN HANCOCK

by Lucia Raatma

Content Adviser: Richard J. Bell, Ph.D.,
Assistant Professor, Department of History,
University of Maryland

Reading Adviser: Alexa L. Sandmann, Ed.D.,
Professor of Literacy, College and Graduate School
of Education, Health and Human Services,
Kent State University

Compass Point Books ✦ Minneapolis, Minnesota

Compass Point Books
151 Good Counsel Drive
P.O. Box 669
Mankato, MN 56002-0669

 This book was manufactured with paper containing
at least 10 percent post-consumer waste.

On the cover: *John Hancock's Defiance,* an 1876 lithograph by Currier & Ives

Photographs ©: The Granger Collection, New York, cover, 5, 10, 18, 28, 30, 31; Robert E. Schafer/iStockpho-
to, 6; Library of Congress, 8, 29, 35; National Portrait Gallery, Smithsonian Institution/Art Resource, NY, 9;
Yale Center for British Art, Paul Mellon Collection, USA/The Bridgeman Art Library, 12; Private Collection/
Peter Newark Pictures/The Bridgeman Art Library, 15; Stock Montage/Getty Images, 16, 19, 21, 36; Private
Collection/The Bridgeman Art Library, 23; Massachusetts Historical Society, Boston, MA, USA/The
Bridgeman Art Library, 25; Hulton Archive/Getty Images, 27; National Archives and Records Administration,
33; National Archives and Records Administration/Our Documents, 37; Michael Latil/National Archives/Time
Life Pictures/Getty Images, 39; U.S. Senate Collection/John Hancock by Horatio Stone, 41.

Editor: Jennifer VanVoorst
Page Production: Heidi Thompson
Photo Researcher: Eric Gohl
Cartographer: XNR Productions, Inc.
Library Consultant: Kathleen Baxter

Art Director: LuAnn Ascheman-Adams
Creative Director: Joe Ewest
Editorial Director: Nick Healy
Managing Editor: Catherine Neitge

Library of Congress Cataloging-in-Publication Data
Raatma, Lucia.
  A signer for independence : John Hancock / by Lucia Raatma.
  p. cm. — (We the People)
  Includes index.
  ISBN 978-0-7565-4122-4 (library binding)
  1. Hancock, John, 1737–1793—Juvenile literature. 2. Statesmen—United States—
Biography—Juvenile literature. 3. United States. Declaration of Independence—Signers—
Biography—Juvenile literature. 4. United States—History—Revolution, 1775–1783—
Juvenile literature. 5. Businessmen—Massachusetts—Boston—Biography—Juvenile literature.
I. Title. II. Title: John Hancock. III. Series.
  E302.6.H23R33 2009
  973.3092—dc22
  [B]   2008035717

Visit Compass Point Books on the Internet at *www.compasspointbooks.com*
or e-mail your request to *custserv@compasspointbooks.com*

Table of Contents

The Famous Signature

*T*he Declaration of Independence is one of the most important documents in the history of the United States. In fact, this document marked the beginning of the new nation. Some very important people signed the declaration. And one signature stands out as bigger and bolder than the rest. That signature is John Hancock's.

In July 1776, the 13 American colonies were still ruled by the government of Great Britain. Many leaders felt that the colonies should break away from the British government and become a free nation. So a group of men was appointed to write a document that would declare the colonies' independence.

John Hancock was president of the Second Continental Congress. This group met in Philadelphia, Pennsylvania, and reviewed the document. Other members of the Continental

Congress included well-known people such as Benjamin

Franklin, Thomas Jefferson, and John Adams.

After suggesting revisions and offering opinions, the

members of the Continental Congress approved the Declaration

of Independence on July 4, 1776. They realized that signing this

paper was a serious matter. It would anger the king of England,

and the signers would be considered traitors to the British

John Hancock's Defiance, *an 1876 lithograph by Currier & Ives*

government. If they were captured by British officials, they would probably be hanged.

But these men did not hesitate. They knew that they had to stand up to the king. John Hancock was the first person to sign the declaration. He did so in big, bold strokes. Then he commented, "There, King George will be able to read that without his spectacles." With this brave act, Hancock proved he was an American patriot.

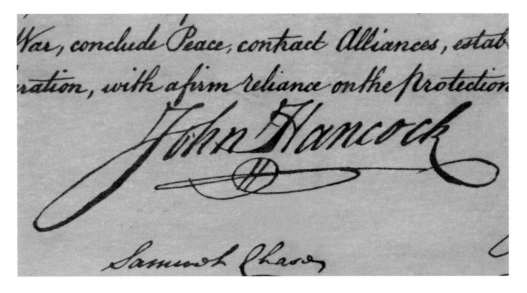

The name "John Hancock" has come to refer to any signature.

2 Growing Up in Massachusetts

John Hancock came from a respected family in the colony of Massachusetts. He was born January 12, 1737, in Braintree, in a section of the city that is now known as Quincy. Both his father and his grandfather were also named John, and they were ministers. His mother, Mary, was the daughter of a farmer. John had a brother, Ebenezer, and a sister, also named Mary.

Braintree was a town about eight miles (13 kilometers) from Boston. Since it was a small village, most people knew one another. John Adams, who would go on to be the second president of the United States, was one of John Hancock's childhood friends.

In his early years, John attended school in Braintree. He played with his friends and went to church. But this seemingly normal life quickly changed when he was just 7 years old. His father died unexpectedly, and the family was left with very little money.

At first, John's grandfather took the family in. He had plans for young John to become a minister as well. However, John's Uncle Thomas offered another solution. He and his wife had no children, so they asked to adopt John. Mary Hancock agreed, and soon her son moved to Boston to live with Thomas and Lydia Hancock.

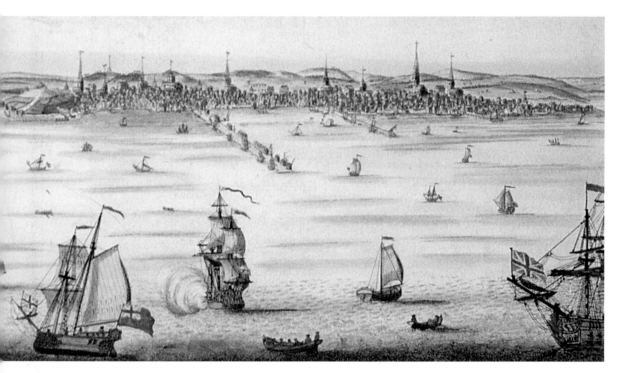

An early 18th-century print of Boston Harbor around the time John Hancock moved there

Thomas Hancock was a wealthy businessman who started out as an apprentice to a bookseller. After learning those skills, he became a book publisher and then went on to create the House of Hancock. This business sold a variety of goods, such as tea, cloth, and paper, to Boston residents. His

Thomas Hancock's portrait was painted by the famous artist John Singleton Copley.

home on Beacon Hill was one of the finest houses in the city.

Living with his aunt and uncle, John was provided with everything he needed. He wore nice clothing, and the family traveled in a beautiful carriage. John attended the Boston Latin School, where he received a fine education.

In those days, young men attended college at an earlier age

The famous patriot Paul Revere made an engraving of Harvard College in 1767.

than most do now. John was just 13 when he was sent to Harvard College in nearby Cambridge. This school, founded in 1636, was the oldest college in the colonies. Approximately 50 young men attended Harvard while John was there. They studied science, philosophy, politics, and classic poetry. The professors encouraged their students to think for themselves and debate one another. When Hancock graduated in 1754, he went to work for his uncle's business. However, he had developed ideas and ways of thinking that stayed with him for years to come.

3

Boston Businessman

*T*he House of Hancock was a thriving business. It owned shops, warehouses, and ships, making it very important in Boston. Under his uncle's leadership, John Hancock quickly learned how the business worked. He came to understand how goods were bought and sold, how accounts were kept, and how to handle profits and losses.

Each morning, John and Thomas Hancock went to work. They dressed in fine clothing, such as wool coats and linen shirts. Each afternoon, the Hancock men would spend hours at the Merchant's Club or at a local tavern or coffeehouse. They knew that entertaining other merchants and having professional contacts were the keys to remaining successful. They would spend time discussing politics and business. And they would enjoy wine and ale, meat, and desserts. John Hancock once said,

A 1720s oil-on-panel painting depicts after-hours business taking place in a tavern.

"The greatest ability in business is to get along with others and to influence their actions." He would use this skill many times during the course of his life.

In 1760, John Hancock traveled to London, England, to live for a few years. The House of Hancock did a lot of business with British merchants, so his uncle wanted him to know these merchants personally. He met and became friends with London businessmen and strengthened the ties between them and the House of Hancock.

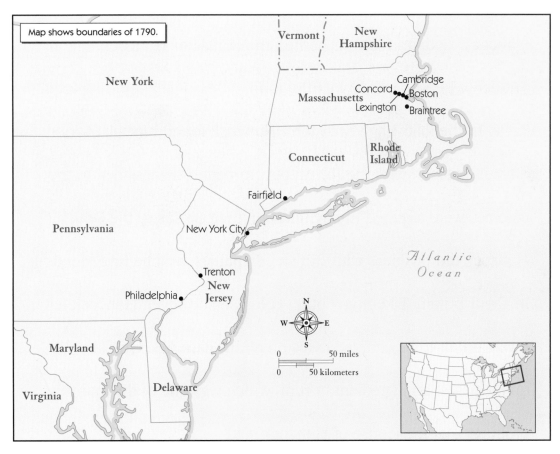

John Hancock lived nearly his entire life in and around the city of Boston, Massachusetts.

When John Hancock returned to Boston, he found that

his uncle had become ill. Thomas was 58 years old, and he no

longer had the energy he once had. On January 1, 1763, John

became a full partner in the House of Hancock and handled

all the day-to-day responsibilities. The following year, Thomas

Hancock died, and John inherited the House of Hancock. Suddenly he was a very wealthy man.

In the following years, John Hancock found himself in a difficult position with the British government. Businessmen in the colonies were required to pay taxes on their profits to the British. Hancock did business with British companies, and he had friends in Great Britain. Like many other colonists, however, Hancock felt it was unfair to be charged taxes on all his earnings. One tax was on molasses, an ingredient in rum, which was one of the many products that the House of Hancock sold.

The Molasses Act stated that American colonists had to buy molasses from the British West Indies, not from other sources, and then pay taxes to Great Britain on any rum sold. Hancock began smuggling molasses so he could avoid paying the taxes. In the meantime, the House of Hancock did business with companies in France and Spain. According to British law, colonial businesses

An 18th-century English lithograph of smugglers loading illegal goods onto their ponies for the journey inland

were supposed to buy most goods only from Britain. Hancock

felt he was best serving his customers by getting the items they

wanted. It was his goal to provide a wide variety of goods

and give his customers fair prices. He also employed a large

number of people, so he felt it was his responsibility to run a

profitable business.

Hancock did not keep all his money to himself. He gave

money to churches and bought the city of Boston a fire engine.

He also donated money, food, and clothing to needy families.

For many years, John Hancock had respected the British government. But as taxes increased, he began to question the laws. He began to believe that American colonies should not have to contribute to the British government if they had no voice in that government. Colonists were not allowed to participate in the British Parliament. Many years before, John Hancock was encouraged at Harvard to think for himself and to debate the issues of the day. As a Boston businessman, he began to use those skills as he faced the problems of British rule.

An 18th-century engraving of the British Parliament in session

4 Facing the British

*T*he tax on molasses was not the only tax charged to the American colonies. Before long, the British government charged taxes on sugar, wine, coffee, silk, and other goods. Officials also realized that some colonial businesses were avoiding the taxes. So they had agents inspect goods coming in and out of American ports.

In 1765, England passed the Stamp Act. This law said that people in the colonies had to buy stamps for all their documents, including books, newspapers, bills, and even college diplomas. This meant that John Hancock had to buy stamps for all the bills he sent to his customers. Newspaper publishers were furious. So were other merchants throughout the colonies.

The colonists began to get very angry. They did not want to pay for stamps or be charged all these taxes. As a result, many

Colonists protested the Stamp Act by burning taxable paper products in the streets.

colonists decided to boycott British goods. At first, Hancock did

not want to take part in the boycott. Before long, however, he

joined the protest.

The British government finally did away with the Stamp Act, but it soon began charging more taxes. There were new taxes on tea, coffee, paint, and cloth. The House of Hancock suffered because many of its customers could not afford British goods anymore. So John Hancock often smuggled other goods—not from Great Britain—into Boston. He also became involved in local politics and began to speak out against the British. He worked with Samuel Adams (cousin of John Adams), James Otis, Thomas Cushing, and other Boston leaders.

Like Hancock, Samuel Adams came to politics by way of business.

At one point, British agents took one of Hancock's ships, the *Liberty*, after Hancock refused to let them search it. They were looking for goods he had not paid taxes on. The British went on to fine Hancock and charged him with smuggling. John Adams served as Hancock's lawyer.

Throughout Boston, people supported John Hancock. They respected him as a smart businessman. They also felt that England's attempt to control colonial businesses was unfair. British soldiers patrolled Boston streets, fearing that the crowds would grow violent. In 1769, colonists again boycotted British goods, and the British government lost a huge amount of money. Eventually charges against Hancock were dropped, but the conflict was far from over.

British soldiers continued to occupy Boston, and the city's people did not like having them there. On March 5, 1770, the tension between the soldiers and the people of Boston erupted in violence, and five Bostonians were killed. The event became

known as the Boston Massacre, and people throughout the

colonies grew even angrier with the British.

The Boston Massacre was one of a series of conflicts that led to the start of the Revolutionary War.

For the next few years, British troops continued to try to control the people of Boston. Samuel Adams and John Hancock formed the Sons of Liberty, a group of patriots who spoke out against the British.

Then, in 1773, Great Britain passed the Tea Act. This law allowed the East India Company to sell tea to colonists without paying taxes on it. Such a law would hurt other tea-selling businesses, such as the House of Hancock. A group of men decided to fight back. On December 16 of that year, the group sneaked onto ships that held tea in Boston Harbor. Dressed as Native Americans, they dumped 342 chests of tea into the water. That tea was worth a great deal of money—equal to what would be $1 million today. This event came to be known as the Boston Tea Party.

John Hancock probably did not participate in the Boston Tea Party, but he likely helped plan it. Afterward, he shipped

An estimated 7,000 angry colonists are believed to have watched the Boston Tea Party.

all his British tea back to Great Britain. He sold his ships and
stopped trading with the British altogether.

In reaction to the Boston Tea Party, the British government

passed a group of laws that colonists called the Intolerable Acts.

These laws, among other things, closed the Boston port and

required colonists to feed and house British soldiers. The soldiers

also set up their tents right on Boston Common, very close to

Hancock's home on Beacon Hill. More and more, the colonists

felt they had no say in what the British government was doing.

The Sons of Liberty and other people throughout the colonies

began to realize it was time to fight for freedom.

The Revolutionary War

As the colonists began to get organized, John Hancock served on the Massachusetts Provincial Congress. He worked to collect weapons and ammunition as the colonies prepared for war against Great Britain. He even had men steal four cannons from the British army. They stored all their supplies in the town of Concord.

The British knew of Hancock's activities, and they considered him a traitor to the

John Hancock played a major role in securing the American colonies' independence from Britain.

king of England. General Thomas Gage, Britain's governor in Massachusetts, realized that Hancock needed to be watched. In April 1775, Gage ordered the arrest of John Hancock and Samuel Adams. Hancock and Adams quickly left Boston and went into hiding in Lexington, a town nearby.

On the night of April 18, 1775, British troops marched toward Lexington and Concord. Their goal was to arrest Hancock and Adams and to find the colonists' supplies. It was on this night that Paul Revere made his famous ride, warning the people of Lexington and Concord that the British soldiers were on the move. William Dawes also spread the message on horseback. Throughout the Massachusetts countryside, Minutemen leapt from their beds and prepared to fight the British. These soldiers earned this nickname because they could be "ready in a minute."

Hancock wanted to face the British, but Adams convinced him that he needed to remain safe. So as the British approached

Lexington, Hancock and Adams fled.

As the morning of April 19 broke, the Minutemen faced the British troops at Lexington. It was a short and confusing battle,

William Barnes Wollen painted Minutemen facing British soldiers on Lexington Common in the first battle of the Revolutionary War.

and no one is completely sure who fired the first shot. But in the end, eight Minutemen were killed and 10 were wounded. Just one British soldier was hurt.

There was a very different outcome in Concord. In the end, 73 British soldiers were killed and 174 were wounded. The supply of weapons had been safely moved and hidden. The British were furious over being defeated. The battles at Lexington and Concord marked the beginning of the Revolutionary War.

As patriots took on British troops throughout the colonies, John Hancock and Samuel Adams traveled to

The Sons of Liberty pulled down a statue of England's King George III after the start of the war.

Philadelphia to attend the Second Continental Congress.

(The First Continental Congress had taken place in 1774.)

They joined other representatives from the colonies, such as

John Adams and George Washington, to plan the war against

Great Britain. Hancock was made president of the Congress,

and he proved to be a good leader. He listened to everyone's

viewpoints and helped all the colonists understand one another.

George Washington (standing) joined John Hancock as one of the leaders of the Second Continental Congress.

George Washington was selected as the commander of the Continental Army. Hancock wanted to join the Army, but he had no military experience. The other men convinced him that he was needed as a businessman instead. So Hancock was put in charge of organizing the troops, getting them supplies, and making sure they were paid. He also purchased 13 ships for the Continental Navy. Since the Army had no money to speak of, Hancock and other wealthy colonists loaned money to the war

On June 19, 1775, John Hancock signed the document that officially made George Washington commander of the Continental Army.

effort. Hancock also arranged a committee to raise funds from

European countries.

As the war continued, Hancock's personal life changed.

He had been seeing Dorothy Quincy (known as Dolly) for

a few years, and the two decided to marry. Their wedding

was on August 28, 1775, in

Fairfield, Connecticut.

Hancock proved

how committed he was

to the patriot cause. The

British troops continued

to occupy Boston,

and some even lived in

Hancock's home. A number

of patriots suggested the

city should be burned so

John Hancock and Dorothy Quincy Hancock

that the soldiers would have to leave. Hancock wrote to Thomas Cushing, "Nearly all the property I have in the world is in houses and other real estate in the town of Boston, but if the expulsion of the British army from it … requires their being burnt to ashes, issue the order for that purpose immediately." Burning Boston was not necessary after all. The British troops finally left and headed to battle in New York City.

By 1776, the situation for the patriots looked grim. The British forces had more troops, more supplies, and more money. That spring, a committee of men from the Continental Congress met to write the Declaration of Independence. The committee members were Thomas Jefferson, Benjamin Franklin, Roger Sherman, John Adams, and Robert Livingston. Jefferson wrote most of the document, and the Congress approved it. Then John Hancock signed his name with the signature that has since become famous.

*The Declaration of Independence is on display
at the National Archives in Washington, D.C.*

Eventually 56 representatives signed the document. It announced to England and the world that the American colonies were independent states.

The remainder of the Revolutionary War was a challenging and difficult time. The British troops won major victories, and the Continental Army became discouraged. But then the patriots won a battle in Trenton, New Jersey, and their hope for independence was renewed.

John and Dolly Hancock suffered a personal loss in 1777 when their baby daughter, Lydia, died of a fever. They were devastated. Further, John Hancock was suffering from gout, which made standing or walking uncomfortable. He decided it was time to leave the Congress.

Hancock returned to Boston and tried to focus on his family life. In 1778, he and Dolly had a son, John George Washington Hancock, whom they called Johnny. In the coming months,

A 1789 engraving of John Hancock's Boston home

Hancock served briefly in the Massachusetts militia. He was

not a skilled military man, and the unit in which he served was

defeated. So Hancock headed back to Boston once again.

6

Governor Hancock

The Revolutionary War was not yet over. The colonies, however, were determined to become an independent nation. So Massachusetts began developing its own constitution and made plans to elect a governor. John Hancock ran for the office, and on September 4, 1780, he won by a huge margin. As governor, Hancock helped to expand the militia, and he worked to build schools and provide children with good educations.

John Hancock was the first governor of the state of Massachusetts.

In 1781, the last battle of the war was finally fought, and the British troops surrendered to the Americans. Two years later, on September 3, 1783, the United States and Great Britain signed the Treaty of Paris. By signing this document, Great Britain recognized the United States as an independent nation. John Hancock and the other signers of the Declaration of Independence were proud of the rebellion they had helped to start.

In the following years, Hancock's health

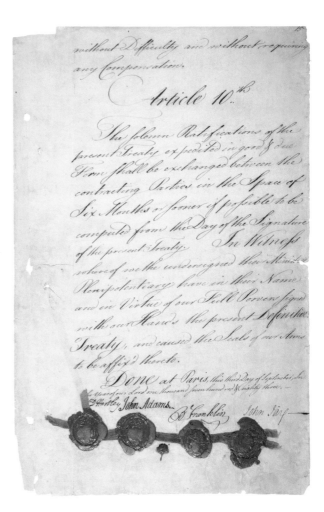

The Treaty of Paris was signed by, among others, Hancock's friend and fellow patriot John Adams.

grew worse. He was re-elected governor in 1784, but he was often too weak to walk or stand. He resigned the position in 1785, deciding to spend more time with his wife and son.

But the Hancocks' quiet family life was shattered again. In January 1787, 8-year-old Johnny fell and hit his head while ice skating on a pond. The injury was so serious that he later died.

John Hancock had a difficult time dealing with his son's death. But he decided that he could not just stay at home and dwell on it. So in the spring of 1788, he once again ran for governor and was elected. One of his biggest tasks was helping Massachusetts ratify the U.S. Constitution. Not everyone agreed with all the details of the Constitution, and Hancock realized that it needed some additions. So he was among the men who helped draft the Bill of Rights, the first 10 amendments to the Constitution. These amendments

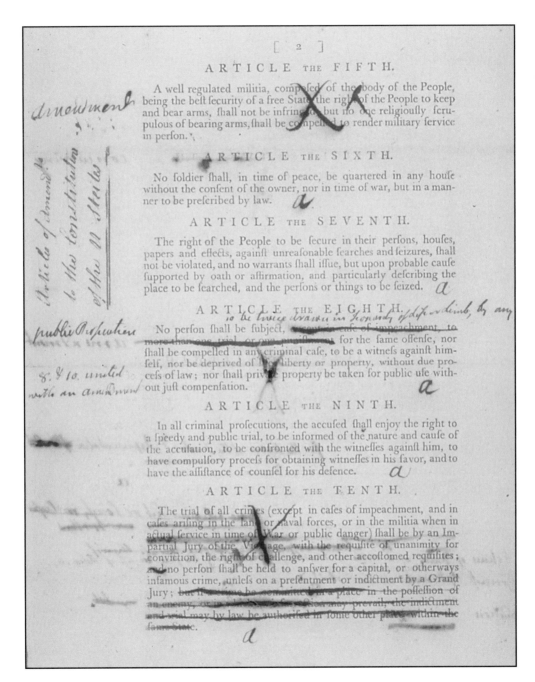

[2]

ARTICLE the FIFTH.

A well regulated militia, composed of the body of the People, being the best security of a free State, the right of the People to keep and bear arms, shall not be infringed; but no one religiously scrupulous of bearing arms, shall be compelled to render military service in person.

ARTICLE the SIXTH.

No soldier shall, in time of peace, be quartered in any house without the consent of the owner, nor in time of war, but in a manner to be prescribed by law.

ARTICLE the SEVENTH.

The right of the People to be secure in their persons, houses, papers and effects, against unreasonable searches and seizures, shall not be violated, and no warrants shall issue, but upon probable cause supported by oath or affirmation, and particularly describing the place to be searched, and the persons or things to be seized.

ARTICLE the EIGHTH.

No person shall be subject, in case of impeachment, to more than one trial or one punishment for the same offense; nor shall be compelled in any criminal case, to be a witness against himself, nor be deprived of life, liberty or property, without due process of law; nor shall private property be taken for public use without just compensation.

ARTICLE the NINTH.

In all criminal prosecutions, the accused shall enjoy the right to a speedy and public trial, to be informed of the nature and cause of the accusation, to be confronted with the witnesses against him, to have compulsory process for obtaining witnesses in his favor, and to have the assistance of counsel for his defence.

ARTICLE the TENTH.

The trial of all crimes (except in cases of impeachment, and in cases arising in the land or naval forces, or in the militia when in actual service in time of War or public danger) shall be by an Impartial Jury of the Vicinage, with the requisite of unanimity for conviction, the right of challenge, and other accustomed requisites; and no person shall be held to answer for a capital, or otherways infamous crime, unless on a presentment or indictment by a Grand Jury; but if a crime be committed in a place in the possession of an enemy, or in which an insurrection may prevail, the indictment and trial may by law be authorised in some other place within the same State.

A draft copy of the Bill of Rights, which was passed by the House of Representatives, shows some changes made in the Senate.

guaranteed citizens the freedom of speech, the freedom of religion, the right to keep and bear arms, and other rights not covered by the original Constitution.

The people of Massachusetts approved of the guarantees of the Bill of Rights, and the state ratified the Constitution. Hancock's ability to help people work together, and his skill of listening to all sides of an issue, again proved to be the key.

When George Washington was chosen as president of the United States, some suggested that Hancock should be his vice president. But Hancock knew his health would not allow him to hold such a position. For the rest of his life he served as governor of Massachusetts. He worked from his home on Beacon Hill. On October 8, 1793, Hancock died at the age of 56. He was serving his ninth term as governor.

Today John Hancock is remembered as one of the Founding Fathers of the United States. He showed his bravery in standing up to the British. He also showed great leadership in the Continental Congress. His business skills helped the American forces win the Revolutionary War and led to the birth of a new nation.

Sculptor Horatio Stone's statue of John Hancock stands in the U.S. Capitol in Washington, D.C.

Glossary

ambush—surprise attack

apprentice—person who works for and learns from a skilled tradesperson for a certain amount of time

Bill of Rights—first 10 amendments to the Constitution; they guarantee freedoms of the press, religion, speech, and others

boycott—refusal to do business with someone as a form of protest

constitution—document stating the basic rules of a government

gout—painful health condition that attacks joints

militia—groups of citizens who have been organized to fight as a group but who are not professional soldiers

Parliament—part of the British government that makes laws

patriot—American colonist who wanted independence from Britain; patriots are people who love their country

ratify—formally approve

smuggling—carrying illegally

traitors—people who betray their country

treaty—formal agreement between groups or nations

Did You Know?

- John Hancock was the only person to sign the Declaration of Independence on July 4, 1776, now celebrated as Independence Day. Most of the other men signed it on August 2.

- Hancock's name on the Declaration of Independence was so important that some people call any signature a John Hancock. For instance, "May I have your John Hancock on this paper?"

- The USS *Hancock* was an aircraft carrier that was in service during World War II (1939–1945) and the Vietnam War (1959–1975).

- The town of Hancock, Massachusetts, is named for John Hancock.

Important Dates

Timeline

1737	Born January 12 in Braintree (now Quincy), Massachusetts
1764	Inherits the House of Hancock
1768	Charged by the British for smuggling; the charges were dropped
1775	Becomes president of the Second Continental Congress; marries Dorothy Quincy
1776	Signs the Declaration of Independence; daughter, Lydia, is born
1777	Lydia dies
1778	Son, John George Washington (Johnny), is born
1780–1785	Serves as governor of Massachusetts
1787	Johnny dies; becomes governor of Massachusetts again
1788	Helps Massachusetts ratify the U.S. Constitution
1793	Dies October 8 in Boston, Massachusetts

Important People

John Adams (1735–1826)

Served under George Washington as the first vice president of the United States and followed him as the second president; he spent nearly 10 years abroad as the first U.S. minister to Great Britain; he died, along with Thomas Jefferson, on July 4, 50 years after the signing of the Declaration of Independence

Samuel Adams (1722–1803)

Patriot who led the opposition to British rule, he was a signer of the Declaration of Independence and a cousin of John Adams; he served as governor of Massachusetts after John Hancock's death

Thomas Jefferson (1743–1826)

Third president of the United States, he served on the committee that wrote the Declaration of Independence and was the main author of that important document; he was also an inventor and created a new kind of plow and improved a device for writing two copies of a letter at once

George Washington (1732–1799)

First saw military action fighting for the British during the French and Indian War (1754–1763); he was named commander of the American forces soon after the Revolutionary War began; he supported a stronger national government and served as the first president of the United States

Want to Know More?

More Books to Read

American Revolution: Battles and Leaders. New York: DK
  Children, 2004.

Fradin, Dennis Brindell. *The Signers: Fifty-Six Stories Behind
  the Declaration of Independence.* New York: Walker &
  Company, 2002.

Gaines, Ann Graham. *John Hancock: President of the Continental
  Congress.* Broomall, Pa.: Chelsea House, 2000.

Raatma, Lucia. *The Battles of Lexington and Concord.*
  Minneapolis: Compass Point Books, 2004.

Ransom, Candice F. *John Hancock.* Minneapolis: Lerner, 2005.

Santella, Andrew. *John Adams.* Minneapolis: Compass Point
  Books, 2002.

On the Web

For more information on this topic, use FactHound.

1. Go to *www.facthound.com*

2. Choose your grade level.

3. Begin your search.

This book's ID number is 9780756541224

FactHound will find the best sites for you.

On the Road

Boston Historical Society
and Museum
Old State House
206 Washington St.
Boston, MA 02109
617/720-1713
Exhibits on the Revolutionary
War and its participants

The National Archives
5700 Pennsylvania Ave. N.W.
Washington, DC 20408
866/272-6272
Display includes the
Declaration of Independence,
the Constitution, and the Bill
of Rights

Look for more We the People Biographies:

American Patriot: Benjamin Franklin

Civil War Spy: Elizabeth Van Lew

Confederate Commander: General Robert E. Lee

Confederate General: Stonewall Jackson

First of First Ladies: Martha Washington

Soldier and Founder: Alexander Hamilton

Union General and 18th President: Ulysses S. Grant

A complete list of We the People titles is available on our Web site:
www.compasspointbooks.com

Index

About the Author

Lucia Raatma loves learning about people's lives and writing about them. In addition to biographies, she has written books about history, safety, animals, and character education. She has a bachelor's degree in English from the University of South Carolina and a master's degree in cinema studies from New York University. When she is not writing or reading, she enjoys going to movies and spending time with her husband, their two children, and their golden retriever.